MW01088146

Confessions of Sin and Assurances of Pardon: A Pocket Resource is a user-friendly guide to the invaluable and oft-neglected practice of confession, and it is a great help to congregations and individuals looking to draw close to God.

John Sowers,
Author and President of The Mentoring Project
Portland, Oregon

Not too long ago, I was surprised to hear that my own faith tradition represents less than 1% of global, historic Christianity. For my own sake and also for the sake of the congregation that I serve, I set out to acquire resources from varying traditions, seasons of history, and theological perspectives within orthodoxy, to enhance our people's understanding that we are part of a pan-national, pan-generational Movement much, much larger than our own tribe and context. Bobby's *Confessions of Sin and Assurances of Pardon* is, in large part, a collection of excerpts from various Christian traditions, and is an outstanding resource – especially for pastors and those who craft liturgy – to connect their worship communities to the broader Church. I highly recommend this book, and plan to use it liberally in my own context.

Scott Sauls
Senior Pastor of Christ Presbyterian Church in Nashville, Tennessee
and author of *Jesus Outside the Lines* and *Befriend*

Pastor Griffith has provided a valuable resource for worship planners and leaders by compiling a significant number of helpful prayers of confession followed by assurances of forgiveness. Jesus taught us in the model Lord's Prayer to cry out to God to forgive our sins and give us a heart of forgiveness toward others. Gathered worship that includes regular prayers of confession forms in us a life of repentance and preaching the gospel to ourselves as we take hold of his kindness that leads to repentance. I commend this work where Pastor Griffith has gathered a wealth of prayers from the rich history of the church and from the present day as well.

Mark Dalbey,
President and Associate Professor of Applied Theology
Covenant Seminary, St. Louis, Missouri

CONFESSIONS OF SIN
AND
ASSURANCES OF PARDON

A POCKET RESOURCE

Bobby G. Griffith Jr.

CHRISTIAN
FOCUS

Bobby Griffith is one of the pastors and founders of City Presbyterian Church in Oklahoma City. He also serves on the board of directors for the foster care organisation, Anna's House Foundation, and teaches History of Christianity at Mid-America Christian University. He and his wife, Jennifer, have one son, Sammy.

Copyright © Bobby G. Griffith Jr., 2016

10 9 8 7 6 5 4 3 2 1

ISBN 978-1-78191-910-1

Published in 2016
by
Christian Focus Publications,
Geanies House, Fearn, Tain, Ross-shire,
IV20 1TW, Scotland, UK

www.christianfocus.com

Cover design by Daniel Van Straaten

Printed and bound by Bookwell, Finland

100%
Paper from well-managed forests
FSC® C041322

PREFACE

A confession is an admission of guilt, an acknowledgment, or profession. In worship Christians have, historically, incorporated confessions of sin as a liturgical practice to invoke the reality that God's people must recognize their need for his grace in their lives. Confessions are a statement that, though God's people are redeemed, they still sin, individually and corporately. Confessions tap into biblical practices seen in the Old and New Testament. They draw the people of God into His great work of redemption.

Confessions often come with a declaration, or assurance of pardon. God promises in His Word that He is ever faithful to forgive. He is the one who gives sinners hope that He casts sin as far as the east from the west. He reminds His people that His steadfast love endures forever. The Apostle John reminds us that He is the faithful one who forgives when we confess our deficiency to answer His great call to love Him with our heart, soul, mind and strength, and to love our neighbor as ourselves.

Because confession and assurance go hand in hand, I have included them in this short book. My intention is to help worship planners and leaders think deeply about leading God's people into the reality of His grace and goodness for His people each and every Lord's Day. Because of this, I employed a wide variety of prayers that follow themes like the Ten Commandments, Seven Deadly Sins, special occasions, and included ancient Christians' prayers as well as biblical ones with a smattering of adaptations from hymns.

I am grateful to my first ministry mentor, the Right Reverend Peter Vaughn, who taught me the importance of crafting beautiful, biblically based worship services. I also appreciate Drs. David Calhoun and Sean Lucas, who instilled a love for church history and taught me to love the rich Christian traditions passed down to us from long ago. Most importantly my wife, Jennifer, and son, Sammy, have shown me the importance of individual confession and my continual need for mercy.

It is in this vein that I, and untold numbers of other Christians, say Jesus, Lamb of God, have mercy. Jesus Bearer of sins, have mercy. Jesus, Redeemer of the world, grant peace. And because God is rich in love, He grants these things through the mighty work of Christ, the Lamb of God who came to take away sin.

Bobby G. Griffith Jr.

FOREWORD

Confessions of Sin in Gospel-Shaped Corporate Worship

One of the first things upon which people remark when they come from other traditions to the Presbyterian church I serve is the time for confession of sin in the order of our Sunday morning worship service. Many of them had never experienced this in the churches from which they had come. Most appreciate an opportunity to reflect meaningfully on their sins and to hear the word of Gospel pardon.

A few, though, have objected: 'It is such a downer to confess sins every week. Why do you do that?' Others have wondered about our use of written confessions spoken corporately: 'I'm not guilty of these sins; why do we have to say this together? Plus, written prayers of confession are simply rote and stale; they don't reflect the issues going on in my heart.' In order to help new Presbyterians understand why we confess our sins in our services week-by-week, we've had to explain a little bit more about the logic of historic Christian worship and how confession fits into that.

Especially since the sixteenth century Reformation, Christian worship serves as a representation of the Gospel as worshipers engage in a covenantal dialogue with their Creator and Redeemer. That's an important sentence that has two ideas. Christian worship serves as a representation of the Gospel: from the call to worship to the benediction, God's people experience a reapplication of the Gospel. The call to worship mirrors effectual calling; the assurance of pardon applies the justifying word once again; the ministry of the Word serves to instruct in new obedience rooted in the Gospel; the benediction assures of God's grace for perseverance. Confession of sin fits into this Gospel representation—as God effectually calls us, renewing our wills, enlightening our minds, we see our sin for what it is and confess it, admitting that we cannot save ourselves. God returns with the word of pardon, reminding us that God in Christ has done all that is necessary to make us right with Him. And so, confession of sin plays an important role each week in reminding us of this Gospel movement.

But Christian worship also engages us in a covenantal dialogue with our Creator and Redeemer. In response to God calling us into worship, we are like Isaiah: we respond with the recognition that we are people with unclean lips and we dwell in the midst of a people of unclean lips. If God does not pardon us, we are utterly undone and lost (Isa. 6:5). The assurance of pardon then comes in response as God speaks; just like the angel of the Lord with Isaiah, there is pardon because there has already been substitution and propitiation. God put forward Jesus to be our substitute, propitiating His wrath and securing pardon for us (Rom. 3:24-25). And so, confession of sin has this vital place in our ongoing covenantal dialogue with God each Lord's Day.

This logic in worship is why Luther, for example, kept the *Kyrie* ('Lord, have mercy') as part of his service. In his Large Catechism, Luther declared, 'When I urge you to go to confession, I am simply urging you to be a Christian.' And elsewhere, he noted that the entire life of believers to be one of repentance (*Ninety-five Theses*). Calvin too had a place for confession of sin early in his worship service. This confession included a strong affirmation of Trinitarian faith as the basis for repentance and hope of pardon. Later in the Genevan service, the Ten Commandments were read with the *Kyrie* sung in response. Like Luther, Calvin knew that confession had to play a significant role in corporate worship if we will grasp and be grasped by the Gospel.

From that Reformation time to our own day, Presbyterian and Reformed worship has sought to 'confess and acknowledge unfeignedly before Your holy majesty that we are poor sinners' (Calvin's liturgy)—not because this is a dour approach to piety or a rote portion of the service. Rather, like the famous Twelve Steps of Alcoholics Anonymous, our weekly confessions of sins allow us to admit the truth: we admit that we are powerless over our lives, that they are unmanageable, and that, unless God saves us through Jesus, we are undone.

And the good news of the Gospel is that 'while we were still sinners, Christ died for us.' Thanks be to God, indeed.

Sean Michael Lucas
Senior Minister, The First Presbyterian Church,
Hattiesburg, Mississippi
Professor of Church History,
Reformed Theological Seminary, Jackson, Mississippi

Jesus, Lamb of God, have mercy on us.
Jesus, Bearer of our sins, have mercy on us.
Jesus, Redeemer of the world, grant us peace.
Amen.

Agnus Dei, the oldest known Christian prayer

002 CONFESSION OF SIN

O Good Shepherd, seek me out, and bring me home to Thy fold again. Deal favorably with me according to Thy good pleasure, till I may dwell in Thy house all the days of my life, and praise Thee for ever and ever with them that are there. Amen.

Jerome (342-420)

O Lord, You who are all merciful, take away my sins from me and enkindle within me the fire of Your Holy Spirit. Take away this heart of stone from me and give me a heart of flesh and blood, a heart to love and adore You, a heart which may delight in You, love You, and please You, for Christ's sake. Amen.

Ambrose of Milan, a 4th Century Bishop

004 CONFESSION OF SIN

O God, cleanse me, a sinner, for I have done nothing good before Thee. Deliver me from the evil one, and may Thy will be in me, that I might open my unworthy lips without condemnation and praise Thy holy name, Father, Son, and Holy Spirit, now and ever and unto ages of ages. Amen.

Macarius (300-391)

O Lord, receive me in repentance; O Lord, leave me not; O Lord, save me from temptation; O Lord, grant me pure thoughts; O Lord, grant me tears of repentance, remembrance of death, and the sense of peace; O Lord, grant me mindfulness to confess my sins; O Lord, grant me humility, charity, and obedience; O Lord, grant me tolerance, magnanimity, and gentleness; O Lord, implant in me the root of all blessings: the fear of Thee in my heart; O Lord, vouchsafe that I may love Thee with all my heart and soul, and that I may obey in all things Thy will; O Lord, shield me from evil persons and devils and passions and all other lawless matters; O Lord, Who knowest Thy creation and that which Thou hast willed for it; may Thy will also be fulfilled in me, a sinner, for Thou art blessed forevermore. Amen.

John Chrysostom

006 CONFESSION OF SIN

Eternal Light, shine into our hearts. Eternal Goodness, deliver us from evil. Eternal Power, be our
support. Eternal Wisdom, scatter the darkness of
our ignorance. Eternal Pity, have mercy upon us,
that with all our heart and mind and soul and
strength we may seek Your face and be brought by
Your infinite mercy to Your holy presence, through
Jesus Christ our Lord. Amen.

Alcuin of York

Grant, Almighty God, that as we are prone to every kind of wickedness and are easily led away to imitate it, when there is any excuse for going astray and any opportunity is offered – O grant, that being strengthened by the help of Thy Spirit, we may continue in purity of faith, and that what we have learned concerning Thee, that Thou art a Spirit, may so profit us, that we may worship Thee in spirit and with a sincere heart, and never turn aside after the corruptions of the world, nor think we can deceive Thee; but may we so devote our souls and bodies to Thee, that our life may in every part of it testify, that we are a pure and holy sacrifice to Thee through Jesus Christ our Lord. Amen.

John Calvin

Behold, Lord, I am an empty vessel that needs to
  be filled. My Lord, fill it.
I am weak in the faith; strengthen me.
I am cold in love; warm me and make me fervent,
  that my love may go out to my neighbor.
I do not have a strong and firm faith; at times
  I doubt and am unable to trust You altogether.
O Lord, help me. Strengthen my faith and trust
  in You.
In You I have sealed the treasure of all I have.
I am poor; You are rich and came to be merciful to
  the poor.
I am a sinner; You are upright.
With me, there is an abundance of sin; in You is the
  fullness of righteousness.
Therefore I will remain with You, of whom I can
  receive, but to whom I may not give. Amen.

Martin Luther

O blessed Jesus, give me stillness of soul in You. Let Your mighty calmness reign in me. Rule me, O King of Gentleness, King of Peace. Amen.

John of the Cross

010 CONFESSION OF SIN

O Father, we are gathered before You, the Maker of Heaven and Earth, whose chosen dwelling place is with the broken and contrite, to confess that we have sinned in thought and word and deed; we have not loved You with all our heart and soul, we have not loved You with all our mind and strength; we have not even loved our neighbor as ourselves. In Your mercy, deepen our sorrow for the wrong we have done and for the good we have left undone, so that we may hate our sin with a holy hatred. But, please, Father, do not leave us in sorrow. With You, O Lord, there is forgiveness. In Your mercy, restore the joy of our salvation; so that we may love You with a holy love. Amen.

From *The Valley of Vision*

Gracious God, our sins are too heavy to carry, too real to hide, and too deep to undo. Forgive what our lips tremble to name, what our hearts can no longer bear, and what has become for us a consuming fire of judgment. Set us free from a past that we cannot change; open to us a future in which we can be changed; and grant us grace to grow more and more in Your likeness and image, through Jesus Christ, the Light of the world. Amen.

Book of Common Worship

Most merciful God, we confess that we have sinned against You in thought, word, and deed, by what we have done, and by what we have left undone. We have not loved You with our whole heart; we have not loved our neighbors as ourselves. We are truly sorry and we humbly repent; for the sake of Your Son Jesus Christ, have mercy on us and forgive us; that we may delight in Your will, and walk in Your ways, to the glory of Your Name. Amen.

The Book of Common Prayer

Holy God, You created us in Your likeness, but through original sin, the image of God was utterly defaced in man, and we became by nature hostile to God, slaves to Satan, and servants to sin. And thus everlasting death has had, and shall have, power and dominion over all who have not been, are not, or shall not be born from above. This rebirth is wrought by the power of the Holy Ghost creating in the hearts of God's chosen ones an assured faith in the promise of God revealed to us in His Word; by this faith we grasp Christ Jesus with the graces and blessings promised in Him. Amen.

The Scots Confession

014 CONFESSION OF SIN

O God, early in the morning I cry to You.
Help me to pray
And to concentrate my thoughts on You:
I cannot do this alone.
In me there is darkness,
But with You there is light;
I am lonely, but You do not leave me;
I am feeble in heart, but with You there is help;
I am restless, but with You there is peace.
In me there is bitterness, but with You there is patience;
I do not understand Your ways,
But You know the way for me ...
Restore me to liberty,
And enable me to live now
That I may answer before You and before me.
Lord, whatever this day may bring,
Your name be praised. Amen.

Dietrich Bonheoffer

Have mercy on me, O God, according to your steadfast love; according to your abundant mercy blot out my transgressions. Wash me thoroughly from my iniquity, and cleanse me from my sin!

For I know my transgressions, and my sin is ever before me. Against you, you only, have I sinned and done what is evil in your sight, so that you may be justified in your words and blameless in your judgment. Behold, I was brought forth in iniquity, and in sin did my mother conceive me. Behold, you delight in truth in the inward being, and you teach me wisdom in the secret heart.

Purge me with hyssop, and I shall be clean; wash me, and I shall be whiter than snow. Let me hear joy and gladness; let the bones that you have broken rejoice. Hide your face from my sins, and blot out all my iniquities. Create in me a clean heart, O God, and renew a right spirit within me. Cast me not away from your presence, and take not your Holy Spirit from me. Restore to me the joy of your salvation, and uphold me with a willing spirit.

Psalm 51:1-12

016 CONFESSION OF SIN

Lord God, You require us to do justice, love mercy and walk humbly before You. We confess that we have not loved You or our neighbor in this way. We repent of this. Grant that Your Holy Spirit drives us to seek these things through Christ. Amen.

Micah 6:8

---

017 CONFESSION OF SIN

I do not understand my own actions. For I do not do what I want, but I do the very thing I hate. Now if I do what I do not want, I agree with the law, that it is good. So now it is no longer I who do it, but sin that dwells within me. For I know that nothing good dwells in me, that is, in my flesh. For I have the desire to do what is right, but not the ability to carry it out. For I do not do the good I want, but the evil I do not want is what I keep on doing. Now if I do what I do not want, it is no longer I who do it, but sin that dwells within me. Deliver me from this body of death through Jesus Christ our Lord. Amen.

Romans 7:15-20

018 CONFESSION OF SIN

Almighty God, who is rich in mercy to all those who call upon You; hear us as we come to You humbly confessing our sins and transgressions, and imploring Your mercy and forgiveness. We have broken Your holy laws by our deeds and by our words, and by the sinful affections of our hearts. Have mercy upon us, most merciful Father; grant that we may hereafter serve and please You in newness of life; through the merit of Jesus Christ our Lord. Amen.

All: Hear our words and our groanings, O Lord. Give attention to our cry for mercy.

Minister: You are not a God who delights in wickedness; evil may not dwell with You. The boastful shall not stand before Your eyes; You hate all evildoers. You destroy those who speak lies; You abhor the bloodthirsty and deceitful.

All: But, O Lord, we are evildoers. We are boastful, deceitful and bloodthirsty.

Minister: By Your mercy alone, by the abundance of Your steadfast love may we enter Your house.

All: Because of Your Son, O Lord, let us find refuge in You. Take away our sins and let us sing for joy. Cover us with Your favor as with a shield. For the sake of our Savior, Jesus Christ. Amen.

Adapted from Psalm 5

020 CONFESSION OF SIN

Merciful God, we confess that we have not
   loved You with our whole heart.
We have failed to be an obedient church.
We have not done Your will,
   we have broken Your law,
   we have rebelled against Your love,
   we have not loved our neighbors,
   and we have not heard the cry of the needy.
Forgive us, we pray.
Free us for joyful obedience,
   through Jesus Christ our Lord. Amen.

From *The Service of Word and Table*, United Methodist Church

021 CONFESSION OF SIN

Jesus, forgive my sins. Forgive the sins that I remember, and the sins I have forgotten. Forgive my many failures in the face of temptation, and those times when I have been stubborn in the face of correction. Forgive the times I have been proud of my own achievements, and when I have failed to boast in Your works. Forgive the harsh judgments I have made of others, and the leniency I have shown myself. Forgive the lies I have told to others, and the truths I have avoided. Forgive me the pain I have caused others and the indulgence I have shown myself. Jesus, have mercy on me and make me whole. Amen.

All-holy Trinity, have mercy on us.
Lord, be gracious to our sins.
Master, pardon our transgressions.
Holy One, visit and heal our infirmities,
for thy Name's sake. Amen.

Traditional Orthodox Confession

All have sinned and fallen short of the glory of God. The hatred which divides nation from nation, race from race, class from class, **Father Forgive.**

The covetous desires of people and nations to possess what is not their own, **Father Forgive.**

The greed which exploits the work of human hands and lays waste the earth, **Father Forgive.**

Our envy of the welfare and happiness of others, **Father Forgive.**

Our indifference to the plight of the imprisoned, the homeless, the refugee, **Father Forgive.**

The lust which dishonors the bodies of men, women and children, **Father Forgive.**

The pride which leads us to trust in ourselves and not in God, **Father Forgive.**

Be kind to one another, tender-hearted, forgiving one another, as God in Christ forgave you.

The Coventry Litany of Reconciliation

024 CONFESSION OF SIN

Eternal God, in whom we live and move and have our being, whose face is hidden from us by our sins, and whose mercy we forget in the blindness of our hearts: cleanse us from all our offenses, and deliver us from proud thoughts and vain desires, that with reverent and humble hearts we may draw near to You, confessing our faults, confiding in Your grace, and finding in You our refuge and strength; through Jesus Christ Your Son.

Confession for the First Commandment

Almighty Father; we enter Your presence confessing the things we try to conceal from You and the things we try to conceal from others. We confess the heartbreak, worry, and sorrow we have caused, that make it difficult for others to forgive us, the times we have made it easy for others to do wrong, the harm we have done that makes it hard for us to forgive ourselves. Lord, have mercy and forgive us through Christ.

Confession for the Second Commandment

Holy God, we have taken Your name in vain every time we have added or taken away from Your character. We have sinned times without number, and been guilty of pride and unbelief, and of neglect to seek You in our daily lives. Our sins and shortcomings present us with a list of accusations, but we thank You that they will not stand against us, for all have been laid on Christ. Deliver us from every evil habit, every interest of former sins, everything that dims the brightness of Your grace in us, everything that prevents us from taking delight in You.

Confession for the Third Commandment

Holy Father, forgive us. Though You should guide us, we inform ourselves. Though You should rule us, we control ourselves. Though You should fulfill us, we console ourselves. For we think Your truth too high, Your will too hard, Your power too remote, Your love too free. But they are not! And without them, we are of all people most miserable. Heal our confused mind with Your Word, heal our divided will with Your law, heal our troubled conscience with Your love, heal our anxious hearts with Your presence, all for the sake of Your Son, who loved us and gave Himself for us. Amen.

Confession for the Fourth Commandment

Jesus, forgive my sins. Forgive the sins that I remember, and the sins I have forgotten. Forgive my many failures in the face of temptation, and those times when I have been stubborn in the face of correction. Forgive the harsh judgments I have made of others, and the leniency I have shown myself. Forgive me for rebelling against the authority structures You've set up in my life. Jesus, have mercy on me and make me thankful for Your rule and reign in my life.

Confession of the Fifth Commandment

Remember, O Lord, Your great mercy and love, for they are from of old. Remember not the sins of my youth, and my rebellious ways: according to Your love remember me, for You are good, O Lord. For the sake of Your name, O Lord, forgive my iniquity, though it is great. Turn to me and be gracious to me, for I am lonely and afflicted. The troubles of my heart have multiplied; free me from my anguish. Look upon my affliction and my distress and take away all my sins.

Confession of the Sixth Commandment

To enrich me will not diminish Your fullness; all Your loving kindness is in Your Son, I bring Him to You in the arms of faith, I urge His saving name as the one who died for me, I plead His blood to pay for my debts of wrong. Accept His worthiness for my unworthiness, His sinlessness for my transgression, His purity for my uncleanness, His sincerity for my guile, His truth for my deceits, His meekness for my pride, His constancy for my backslidings, His love for my enmity, His fullness for my emptiness, His faithfulness for my treachery, His obedience for my lawlessness, His glory for my shame, His devotedness for my waywardness, His holy life for my unchaste ways, His righteousness for my dead works, His death for my life.

Confession for the Seventh Commandment

O Lord, my every sense, member and affection, is a snare to me. I can scarce open my eyes but I envy those above me, or despise those below. I covet the honor and riches of the mighty, and am proud and unmerciful to the rags of others. If I behold beauty it is a bait to lust; or see deformity, it stirs up loathing and disdain. How soon do slanders and wanton speeches creep into my heart! You know that all these are snares by my corruptions, and that my greatest snare is myself. Keep me ever mindful of my natural state, but let me not forget my heavenly title, or the grace that can deal with every sin.

Confession for the Eighth Commandment

Merciful Lord, we confess that with us there is an abundance of sin, but in You there is the abundance of mercy. We are spiritually poor, but You are rich and in Jesus Christ came to be merciful to the poor. Strengthen our faith in You. We are empty vessels that need to be filled; fill us. We are weak in faith; strengthen us. We are cold in love; warm us, that our love may go out to one another and to our neighbors. Through Jesus Christ our Lord.

Confession for the Ninth Commandment

Lord Jesus Christ, sin is my malady, my monster, my foe, my viper, born in my birth, alive in my life, strong in my character, dominating my faculties, following me as a shadow, intermingling with my every thought, my chain that holds me captive. Yet Your compassions yearn over me, Your heart hastens to my rescue, Your love endured my curse, Your mercy bore my justice. Let me walk in humility, bathed in Your blood, tender of conscience, living in triumph as an heir of salvation through Your blessed name.

Confession for the Tenth Commandment

Lord God, in this season we are reminded that You became flesh and dwelt among humanity with perfect love for God and perfect love for neighbor. You entered into this world and the lives of others to bring light and life. We confess that, at times, we have neglected God and others. We confess that we have not entered into the lives of others in love. We repent of these sins and come to You in confidence, knowing Your steadfast love for us endures forever. In the name of Christ, we pray, Amen.

A General Confession during Advent or Christmas

Leader: God forgives and heals us.

All: We need Your healing, merciful God. Give us true repentance. Some sins are plain to us, some escape us, some we cannot face. Forgive us. Set us free to hear Your Word to us. Set us free to serve You.

Leader: God forgives you. Forgive others. Forgive yourself.

A New Zealand Prayer Book

5/10/20

036 CONFESSION OF SIN

Holy Father, You see us as we are and know our inmost thoughts. We confess that we are unworthy of Your gracious care. We forget that all life comes from You and that to You all life returns. We have not sought to do Your will with our whole hearts. We have not lived as grateful children, nor lived as Christ loves us. Apart from You, we are nothing. Only Your grace can sustain us. Lord, in Your mercy, forgive us, heal us, and make us whole. Set us free from our sin and restore us to the joy of Your salvation now and evermore. Amen.

Lord, forgive us of our sins. Wash us in Your Word. Turn our hearts of stone into hearts of flesh. Give us ears that we may hear, and eyes that we may see. Perfect that concerning us and make us whole. For we have failed to love You with our whole hearts. We have turned to our own way. We are lost without You. Lead us in the paths of righteousness for Your name's sake. May Your Word be a lamp unto our feet and a light unto our pathway. Order our steps and stops for Your glory. Grant us a worthy walk, holy habits, devoted discipleship, consistent compassion, and liberated love, that we may perfectly love You. In Jesus' name, Amen.

Rev. C. J. Rhodes

O Holy One, we call to You and name You as eternal, ever-present, and boundless in love. Yet there are times, O God, when we fail to recognize You in the dailyness of our lives. Sometimes shame clenches tightly around our hearts, and we hide our true feelings. Sometimes fear makes us small, and we miss the chance to speak from our strength. Sometimes doubt invades our hopefulness, and we degrade our own wisdom.

Holy God, in the daily round from sunrise to sunset, remind us again of Your holy presence hovering near us and in us. Free us from shame and self-doubt. Help us to see You in the moment-by-moment possibilities to live honestly, to act courageously, and to speak from our wisdom.

Almighty God, who does freely pardon all who repent and turn to Him, now fulfill in every contrite heart the promise of redeeming grace; forgiving all our sins, and cleansing us from an evil conscience; through the perfect sacrifice of Christ Jesus our Lord. Amen.

Book of Common Worship

040 CONFESSION OF SIN

Almighty God, since Thou delayest with so much forbearance the punishments which we have deserved and daily draw on ourselves, grant that we may not indulge ourselves but carefully consider how often and in how many different ways we have provoked Thy wrath against us. May we learn humbly to present ourselves to Thee for pardon, and with true repentance implore Thy mercy. With all our heart we desire to submit ourselves to Thee, whether Thou chastisest us, or according to Thine infinite goodness, forgivest us. Let our condition be ever blessed, not by flattering ourselves in our apathy, but by finding Thee to be our kind and bountiful Father, reconciled to us in Thine only-begotten Son. Amen.

John Calvin from *Prayers of the Reformers*

Holy God and Creator of all that is, we confess to You that we have sinned. We have failed in our care for the land and its creatures. We have been greedy, destructive and wasteful of the resources You have entrusted to us. We have polluted the air and water, eroded the soil and earth, deprived the birds and animals, and hurt our neighbors by our selfishness. All these cry out against us. Most of all we have either neglected or forgotten our worship of You as our Creator and Redeemer. Forgive us for turning our back on You and not acknowledging You. We use Your creation, and so we use You.

Forgive us, we pray, and have mercy. Give us grace to change our ways, to make amends, and to work together for the healing of the world, through Jesus Christ our Lord. May we see You as Lord of all, and of our hearts and lives, and may we worship You. Amen.

Adapted from the Anglican General Council

042 CONFESSION OF SIN

Almighty Father; we enter Your presence confessing the things we try to conceal from You and the things we try to conceal from others. We confess the heartbreak, worry, and sorrow we have caused, that make it difficult for others to forgive us, the times we have made it easy for others to do wrong, the harm we have done that makes it hard for us to forgive ourselves. Lord, have mercy and forgive us through Christ. Amen.

Save Your people, God of truth and mercy, from the chaos of divided loyalties and the worship of many gods; Save us, God of truth and mercy. From making God in our own likeness and the slavery of self-centeredness; Save us, God of truth and mercy. From using God's name trivially and claiming Him for our prejudices; Save us, God of truth and mercy. From neglecting sabbatical quiet times and being obsessed with busyness; Save us, God of truth and mercy. From ignoring or despising the elderly and over-indulging the new generation; Save us, God of truth and mercy. From glorifying armaments and war and wishing our enemies dead; Save us, God of truth and mercy. From watering-down love and marriage, and the exploitation of sex; Save us, God of truth and mercy. From the legal robberies of the stock exchange, and the cunning thefts of tax evasion; Save us, God of truth and mercy. From TV programmes that twist the facts, and cruel gossip in supermarkets; Save us, God of truth and mercy. From those who preach greed as a virtue and possession a lust which is never satisfied; Save us, God of truth and mercy. O Jesus Christ, Savior of all who lose their way, O Healing Spirit, Power who renews the world; We need You, God of truth and mercy! Amen!

From 'Prayers For the Twenty-First Century' © Bruce Prewer and Open Book Publishers

Almighty God, You have raised Jesus from death to life, and crowned Him Lord of all. We confess that we have not bowed before Him, or acknowledged His rule in our lives. We have gone along with the ways of the world, and failed to give Him glory. Forgive us and raise us from sin, that we may be Your faithful people, obeying the commands of our Lord Jesus Christ, who rules the world and is head of the Church, His body. In His name we pray, Amen.

Traditional Reformed Confession

We confess to You, Lord, what we are: we are not the people we like others to think we are; we are afraid to admit even to ourselves what lies in the depths of our souls. But we do not want to hide our true selves from You. We believe that You know us as we are, and yet You still love us. Help us not to shrink from self-knowledge; teach us to respect ourselves for Your sake; give us the courage to put our trust in Your guiding power. Raise us out of the paralysis of guilt and fear and take us into the freedom and energy of forgiven people. And for those who through long habit find forgiveness hard to accept, we ask that You would break their bondage and set them free. Through Jesus Christ we pray, Amen.

The Covenant Hymnal

Merciful God, we confess to You now that we have sinned. We confess the sins that no one knows and the sins that everyone knows.

We confess the sins that are a burden to us
and the sins that do not bother us
because we have grown used to them.

We confess our sins as a church.

We have not loved one another as Christ loved us. We have not forgiven one another as we have been forgiven. We have not given ourselves in love and service for the world as Christ gave Himself for us.

Father, forgive us. Send the Holy Spirit to us,
That He may give us power to live as, by Your mercy,
You have called us to live. Through Jesus Christ our Lord, Amen.

Holy and merciful God, in Your presence we confess our sinfulness, our shortcomings, and our offenses against You. You alone know how often we have sinned in wandering from Your ways, in wasting Your gifts, in forgetting Your love. Have mercy on us, O Lord, for we are ashamed and sorry for all we have done to displease You. Forgive our sins, and help us to live in Your light, and walk in Your ways, for the sake of Jesus Christ our Savior. Amen.

The Service for the Lord's Day: The Worship of God

Eternal God, our Judge and Redeemer, we confess that we have tried to hide from You, for we have done wrong. We have lived for ourselves and apart from You. We have turned from our neighbors and refused to bear the burdens of others. We have ignored the pain of the world, and passed by the hungry, the poor, and the oppressed. In Your great mercy forgive our sins and free us from selfishness, that we may choose Your will and obey Your commandments; through Jesus Christ our Savior. Amen.

God of mercy, You sent Jesus Christ to seek and save the lost. We confess that we have strayed from You and turned aside from Your way. We are misled by pride, for we see ourselves pure when we are stained, and great when we are small. We have failed in love, neglected justice, and ignored Your truth. Have mercy, O God, and forgive our sin. Return us to paths of righteousness through Jesus Christ, our Savior. Amen.

Book of Common Worship

God of grace and truth, in Jesus Christ You came among us as light shining in darkness. We confess that we have not welcomed the light, or trusted good news to be good. We have closed our eyes to glory in our midst, expecting little, and hoping for less. Forgive our doubt and renew our hope, so that we may receive the fullness of Your grace and live in the truth of Christ the Lord. Amen.

Book of Common Worship

O Almighty God, merciful Father, I, a poor, miserable sinner, confess unto Thee all my sins and iniquities with which I have ever offended Thee and justly deserved Thy temporal and eternal punishment. But I am heartily sorry for them and sincerely repent of them, and I pray Thee of Thy boundless mercy and for the sake of the holy, innocent, bitter sufferings and death of Thy beloved Son, Jesus Christ, to be gracious and merciful to me, a poor, sinful being. Amen.

From *The Lutheran Hymnal*, 1941

Almighty God, our Maker and Redeemer, we poor sinners confess unto thee, that we are by nature sinful and unclean, and that we have sinned against thee by thought, word, and deed. Wherefore we flee for refuge to thine infinite mercy, seeking and imploring thy grace, for the sake of our Lord Jesus Christ.

From the *Lutheran Service Book and Hymnal,* 1958

Holy God, we confess that we are not worthy of the riches of life for which the generations of men have labored that we might enter into this heritage. We confess the sorry confusion of our common life, the greed which disfigures our collective life and sets man against his fellowmen. We confess the indifference and callousness with which we treat the sufferings and insecurity of the poor, and the pettiness which mars relations between us. May we with contrite hearts seek once more to purify our spirits through Jesus Christ our Lord, who lives and reigns with You and the Holy Spirit, one God, now and forever more.

Adapted from a confession written by Reinhold Niebuhr

God, You ask for our courage to protect the power-less but we prefer to remain safe, preserving our-selves for future challenges. You ask us to speak out for justice but we whisper, in case we are heard. You ask us to stand up for what is right, but we would rather blend in to the crowd. You ask us to have faith, when doubting seems so much easier. Lord, forgive our calculated efforts to follow You, only when it is convenient to do so, only in those places where it is safe to do so, only with those who make it easy to do so. God, forgive us and renew us; Inspire us and challenge us so that we might risk the journey, to Your kingdom with You. Amen.

A prayer from Kairos South Africa, 2003

Eternal and merciful God, You have loved us with a love beyond our understanding, and You have set us on paths of righteousness for Your name's sake. Yet, we have strayed from Your way; we have sinned against You in thought, word, and deed, through what we have done and what we have left undone, and we have wandered from Your pathway. As we remember the cleansing water of baptism, O God, we praise You and give You thanks that You forgive us yet again. Grant us now, we pray, the grace to die daily to sin, and to rise daily to new life in Christ, who lives and reigns with You, and in whose strong name we pray. Amen.

A confession on the occasion of baptism, adapted from John Calvin by _Reformed Worship_

Give me a clean heart so I may serve Thee.
Lord, fix my heart so that I may be used by Thee,
For I'm not worthy of all these blessings.
Give me a clean heart, and I'll follow thee.

I'm not asking for the riches of this land,
And I'm not asking for men in high places to
  know my name.
Please give me, Lord, a clean heart that I may
  follow Thee.
Give me a clean heart, and I'll follow Thee.

Give me a Clean Heart by **Margaret Douroux**

We confess to You, Gracious God, that too often we look on Your law as a burden, not a gift; an inconvenience, not a blessing. Rather than seeing Your love revealed, we feel our own guilt magnified. Instead of rejoicing in Your good news, we focus on our own shortcomings. Turn us around, Redeemer, and do not let our fears have dominion over us. Enlighten us, so that our words and deeds may be acceptable to You. Amen.

Based on Nehemiah 8:1-10 in the United Church of Christ, *Worship Ways Archive*

Almighty, eternal God and Father, we confess and acknowledge unto You that we were conceived in unrighteousness and are full of sin and transgression in all our life. We do not fully believe Your Word nor follow Your holy commandments. Remember Your goodness, we beseech You, and for Your Name's sake be gracious unto us, and forgive us our iniquity which, alas, is great. Amen.

Martin Bucer

O Lord God, eternal and almighty Father, we confess and sincerely acknowledge before Your holy Majesty that we are poor sinners, conceived and born in iniquity and corruption, prone to do evil, incapable of any good, and that in our depravity we transgress Your holy commandments without end or ceasing; therefore we purchase for ourselves, through Your righteous judgment, our ruin and perdition. Nevertheless, O Lord, we are grieved that we have offended You, and we condemn ourselves and our sins with true repentance, beseeching Your grace to relieve our distress. O God and Father, most gracious and full of compassion, have mercy upon us in the name of Your Son, our Lord Jesus Christ. And as You do blot out our sins and stains, magnify and increase in us day by day the grace of Your Holy Spirit; that as we acknowledge our unrighteousness with all our heart, we may be moved by that sorrow which shall bring forth true repentance in us, mortifying all our sins, and producing in us the fruits of righteousness and innocence which are pleasing to You, through Jesus Christ our Lord. Amen.

Strasbourg Liturgy, 1545

Almighty God, Father of our Lord Jesus Christ, Maker of all things, Judge of all men; we acknowledge and bewail our manifold sins and wickedness, which we, from time to time, most grievously have committed, by thought, word, and deed, against Thy Divine Majesty, provoking most justly Thy wrath and indignation against us. We do earnestly repent, and are heartily sorry for these our misdoings; the remembrance of them is grievous unto us; the burden of them is intolerable. Have mercy upon us, have mercy upon us, most merciful Father; for Thy Son our Lord Jesus Christ's sake, forgive us all that is past; and grant that we may ever hereafter serve and please Thee in newness of life, to the honour and glory of Thy Name; through Jesus Christ our Lord. Amen.

Book of Common Prayer, 1552

Almighty God, eternal Father, we acknowledge and confess to You that we were born in unrighteousness. Our life is full of sin and transgression; we have not gladly believed Your Word nor followed Your holy commandments. For your goodness' sake and for Your name's sake, be gracious unto us, we pray, and forgive us all our sin, which is very great. Amen.

From a 1539 liturgy used by both John Calvin and John Knox

Lord, we confess that we are debtors in need of Your grace. May Your grace bind our wandering hearts to You because we are prone to wander, we feel it. We are prone to leave You, the one we love. Here are our hearts, take and seal them for the sake of Christ. Amen.

Adapted from *Come Thou Fount of Every Blessing* **by Robert Robinson.**

Lord, You are our Shepherd, yet we still want. You promise us rest, but we refuse to be still. You are our Righteousness, but we look to our own works. You are with us, but yet we still fear and do not trust Your promises of protection and cower at our enemies. Lord, forgive us. Cause us to embrace Your goodness and mercy that we may truly believe that You will be with us all the days of our life. We pray this in the name of Christ. Amen.

Adapted from Psalm 23

Lord, our hearts are restless.
They are deceitful and full of wickedness.
Yet You are gracious because of Christ.

Lord, we ask that our hearts find their rest in You.
Here are our hearts, Lord. We offer them to You,
promptly and sincerely, for the sake of Your Son.
Amen.

Adapted from Augustine, Jeremiah 17:9 and John Calvin's motto

Lord, we confess that sometimes when others have what we do not have, we burn! We begin to tell ourselves and others around us that life has been unfair to us. We fail to rejoice in the blessing others have received, and we fail to rejoice in the unique blessings we have received. We instead covet someone else's blessing for ourselves, and in doing so fail to acknowledge that all good things come from You.

Lord, though envy has gripped us, we confess our need to walk in a new way. We ask You to lead us in a new way. And as we seek to walk in this new way we repent of this sin of envy. We turn from this wickedness of our hearts. We choose to walk instead in the way of love, with Your help. Teach us and move in our hearts to love You and to love our neighbor as we ought, and to forsake this sin of envy. May it be far from us, Lord. Through the power of Christ working in us we pray. Amen.

A Confession for the Sin of Envy

Lord, we confess to You our sin of greed. We confess that we have tried to serve two masters. We have said that we love You, but our actions have displayed a love of worldly possessions instead. Our selfish greed has consumed time and attention that should have gone to those we love. It has squandered resources that should have been given to those in need. It has stolen the tithes and offerings and acts of devotion that should have been Yours. We ask You, Lord, to forgive us of our greed and self-centeredness. Search our hearts and show us where we have been blind to our sin. Bring us to repentance and cleanse us, so that we will serve You and others, with undivided hearts. In the name of Jesus Christ our Lord we pray. Amen.

A Confession for the Sin of Greed

Lord, we confess to You our sin of anger. We confess that we have violated Your command not to let the sun go down while we are angry. We confess that our anger has brought harm to others, that it has grieved the Holy Spirit, that it has corrupted our prayers and worship, and that it has prevented us from living lives that are righteous in Your sight. We ask You, Lord, to cleanse us of our anger and to give us the grace instead to be quick to listen, slow to speak, and slow to become angry, because our anger does not bring about the righteous life that You desire for us. Lord, lead us in that way of righteousness and cleanse us for Your name's sake. In the name of Jesus Christ our Lord, we pray. Amen.

Confession for the Sin of Anger

Lord, as those who live in a nation in which obesity has become epidemic, we confess to You our sin of gluttony. Whether collectively or individually, we confess that we have turned to food and drink where we should have found our satisfaction with You instead. We have taken Your gifts of sustenance and provision, and placed them above You on the altar of our hearts. We have eaten and drunk to excess, seeking to be satisfied. And yet we will not be satisfied, because we have failed to find our satisfaction fully in You. We ask You, Lord, to help us in our weakness. May we receive Your blessings of provision with thankfulness. May we be good stewards of what You have provided and of our bodies for which that provision is made. May we have hearts that worship You fully as the Provider. May we consume what we eat and what we drink in the moderation that comes from trusting You and from desiring Your pleasure in our lives. In the name of our Lord Jesus we ask this. Amen.

Confession for the Sin of Gluttony

Lord, Your Word speaks of the lazy person with disdain: The sluggard imagines a lion in the streets as an excuse for not venturing out. The sluggard turns on his bed like a door turns on its hinges. The sluggard buries his hand in the dish, but is too lazy to bring it back to his mouth. The sluggard is wiser in his own eyes than seven who answer discreetly. There is more hope for a fool than for such a person.

Lord, we confess our tendency toward laziness. We confess that we waste precious time that could be spent serving You and others. We confess that our idleness easily leads us to other sins. We acknowledge that when we behave in this way we fail to live under Your lordship in our lives.

May such idleness and all its ill effects be far from us! May we work appropriately and live productive lives before You and others, as You lead us through Your strength. We pray this in the able name of our Lord and Master Jesus Christ. Amen.

Confession for the Sin of Sloth

Lord, we live in a world in which lust is exalted as a virtue rather than acknowledged as sin. Promiscuity is encouraged. Adultery is excused. Indecency is mass-marketed. Perversion is championed as normal behavior. Precious human beings are exploited for destructive, wickedly indulgent purposes. We confess that we as fallen human beings are too easily tempted by the lust of the flesh. We confess that we are prone to the same types of behavior that have lured the world away from You and from Your desire for purity and chastity. We confess that in our sin of lust we have exchanged Your truth for a lie and have worshipped created things, placing them above You, our Creator. Cleanse us with hyssop, and we will be clean. Wash us, and we will be whiter than snow. Turn Your face from our sins and blot out all our iniquity. Create in us a pure heart, O God, and renew a steadfast spirit within us. Do not cast us from Your presence or take Your Holy Spirit from us. Restore to us the joy of Your salvation and grant us willing spirits, to sustain us. We offer our bodies to You as a living sacrifice, asking You to transform us by the renewing of our minds and hearts. We ask You to wash away our sin and help us to walk in newness of life. In the name of Jesus and through His cleansing blood we ask this. Amen.

Confession for the Sin of Lust

Lord, we confess that we do not see ourselves as we ought. We are excessively confident in our own sufficiency. We habitually trust our own wisdom. We constantly overestimate our abilities, our resources, and our strength. We fail to acknowledge that in reality we are weak, poor, wretched, and blind. In our ignorance of the truth we deprive ourselves of Your grace, of Your strength in our weakness, and of Your sufficiency for the many ways in which we are lacking.

Lord, we confess to You our sin of pride. We humble ourselves before You. We acknowledge our desperate need of You. We ask that, by the power of Your Holy Spirit, You will help us see ourselves as You see us. Help us to know fully our constant need for You. And may we walk in Your grace, Your strength, and Your sufferings. We pray, in the name of Jesus. Amen.

Confession for the Sin of Pride

072 CONFESSION OF SIN

Almighty God, have mercy on us, forgive us all our sins through our Lord Jesus Christ, strengthen us in all goodness, and by the power of the Holy Spirit keep us in eternal life. Amen.

The Book of Common Prayer

Our ever merciful and compassionate God, forgive our forgetfulness of Your grace to us. We, from time to time, have demanded of others a standard that we have failed to meet ourselves. We have related to others in terms of measuring up to this standard, rather than as fellow debtors to grace. We have forgotten the profundity of our need, and thought of ourselves as worthy of Your favor, and so have demeaned others in thought, word and deed. O Lord, our Savior, show us again the depth and breadth of Your marvelous work on our behalf, that we may evermore, all the days of our lives, express an ever increasing understanding of Your gospel, in our relationship to You, and others, through the power of Your Spirit at work in us, in the name of Your blessed Son, Amen.

Holy God, You said that You are the Light of the World, yet we still refuse to let You into the darkest places of our lives. You said that You are the Good Shepherd, but we fail to follow where You lead. We are sheep that have gone astray. You said that You are the bread of life, but we seek out other things to satisfy us. You said that You are the Way, but we often make our own paths. You said that You are the Truth, but we find ways to deceive ourselves and others. You said that You are Life. Forgive us and help us to embrace the mercy, forgiveness, and grace that You offer us so that we can have an abundant life with You. In Jesus' Name we pray, Amen.

From a 2016 liturgy of Memorial Drive Presbyterian Church

Most merciful God, whose Son Jesus Christ was tempted in every way, yet without sin, we confess before You our own sinfulness; we have hungered after that which does not satisfy; we have compromised with evil; we have doubted Your power to protect us. Forgive us for our lack of faith; have mercy on our weakness. Restore us in such trust and love that we may walk in Your ways and delight in doing Your will. We ask in Jesus' name. Amen.

Traditional Reformed Confession of Sin

076 CONFESSION OF SIN

Forgive the sins I have confessed to Thee;
forgive the sins I do not see;
O guide me, love me, and my keeper be.
Dear Lord, forgive.

C.M. Battersby

Loving Father,
Be merciful and forgive our sin.
Cleanse our unrighteousness.
Heal our hurts, and reconcile our broken relationships.
Pour Your Spirit upon us with renewing grace.
Restore to us the 'joy of our salvation'.
Forgive our excessiveness and ingratitude.
Make us a thankful people with charitable hearts,
Who drink from the well of Your grace,
That this broken world will taste
The new wine of the gospel.
Through Jesus, Amen.

Rev. Mike Khandjian

Pastor: God our Father, You sent Your Son full of grace and truth: forgive our failure to receive Him. Lord, have mercy.

All: Lord, have mercy.

Pastor: Jesus our Savior, You were born in poverty and laid in a manger: forgive our greed and rejection of Your ways. Christ, have mercy.

All: Christ, have mercy.

Pastor: Spirit of Love, Your servant Mary responded joyfully to Your call: forgive the hardness of our hearts. Lord, have mercy.

All: Lord, have mercy.

Book of Common Prayer

By faith, we have peace with God through our Lord Jesus Christ.

Romans 5:1

The LORD is gracious and merciful,
   slow to anger and abounding in steadfast love.
The LORD is good to all,
   and his mercy is over all that he has made.

Psalm 145:8-9

May the God of all healing and forgiveness draw you to Himself and cleanse you from all your sins, that you may behold the glory of His Son, the Word made flesh, Jesus Christ our Lord. Amen.

Common Worship: Times and Seasons

082 ASSURANCE OF PARDON

If you, O LORD, should mark iniquities,
  O Lord, who could stand?
But with you there is forgiveness,
  that you may be ~~revered~~. *feared,*

Psalm 130:3-4

In him we have redemption through his blood, the forgiveness of our trespasses, according to the riches of his grace, which he lavished upon us, in all wisdom and insight making known to us the mystery of his will, according to his purpose, which he set forth in Christ as a plan for the fullness of time, to unite all things in him, things in heaven and things on earth.

Ephesians 1:7-10

The LORD is merciful and gracious,
   slow to anger and abounding in steadfast love.
He will not always chide,
   nor will he keep his anger forever.
He does not deal with us according to our sins,
   nor repay us according to our iniquities.
For as high as the heavens are above the earth,
   so great is his steadfast love toward those
   who fear him;
as far as the east is from the west,
   so far does he remove our transgressions from us.

Psalm 103:8-12

---

085 ASSURANCE OF PAR_____

Hear the comforting words of Jesus for those who come to him with their nothing: 'Blessed are the poor in spirit, for theirs is the kingdom of heaven.' Brothers and sisters, the pardon of Christ is a grace that is greater than all our sin. You are forgiven.

Matthew 5:3

Behold, the LORD has proclaimed
   to the end of the earth:
Say to the daughter of Zion,
   'Behold, your salvation comes;
behold, his reward is with him,
   and his recompense before him.'
And they shall be called The Holy People,
   The Redeemed of the LORD;
and you shall be called Sought Out,
   A City Not Forsaken.

Isaiah 62:11-12

As for you, O LORD, you will not restrain
   your mercy from me;
your steadfast love and your faithfulness will
   ever preserve me!

Psalm 40:11

Now the Lord is the Spirit, and where the Spirit of the Lord is, there is freedom. And we all, with unveiled face, beholding the glory of the Lord, are being transformed into the same image from one degree of glory to another. For this comes from the Lord who is the Spirit.

Christian, you are free in Christ. Rest in the freedom of His forgiveness.

2 Corinthians 3:17-18

For with you is the fountain of life;
in your light do we see light.

Psalm 36:9

The LORD your God is in your midst,
    a mighty one who will save;
he will rejoice over you with gladness;
    he will quiet you by his love;
he will exult over you with loud singing.

Zephaniah 3:17

Righteousness will be counted to us who believe in him who raised from the dead Jesus our Lord, who was delivered up for our trespasses and raised for our justification.

Romans 4:24-25

092 ASSURANCE OF PARDON

He has delivered us from the domain of darkness and transferred us to the kingdom of his beloved Son, in whom we have redemption, the forgiveness of sins.

Colossians 1:13-14

In the beginning was the Word, and the Word was with God, and the Word was God. He was in the beginning with God. All things were made through him, and without him was not any thing made that was made. In him was life, and the life was the light of men. The light shines in the darkness, and the darkness has not overcome it.

John 1:1-5

Comfort, comfort my people, says your God.
Speak tenderly to Jerusalem,
  and cry to her
that her warfare is ended,
  that her iniquity is pardoned,
that she has received from the LORD's hand
  double for all her sins.

Isaiah 40:1-2

She will bear a son, and you shall call his name Jesus, for he will save his people from their sins.

Children of God, Jesus saves you from your sins. Walk in His salvation, today and evermore.

Matthew 1:21

096 ASSURANCE OF PARDON

The mercy of the Lord is from everlasting to everlasting. May the God of mercy, who forgives us all our sins, strengthen us in all goodness, and by the power of the Holy Spirit keep us in eternal life. Amen.

Book of Common Prayer

If we confess our sins, he is faithful and just to forgive us our sins and to cleanse us from all unrighteousness.

Brothers and sisters, by the command of Christ and the power of his promises, you are forgiven.

I John 1:9

For God so loved the world, that he gave his only begotten Son, that whosoever believeth in him should not perish, but have everlasting life. (KJV)

John 3:16

Christ died for our sins. He made a full atonement for us. We are forgiven and we have the promise of eternal life. Feel that forgiveness in your heart. We are His children. Amen.

100 ASSURANCE OF PARDON

Who has believed what he has heard from us?
    And to whom has the arm of the Lord been revealed?
For he grew up before him like a young plant,
    and like a root out of dry ground;
he had no form or majesty that we should look at him,
    and no beauty that we should desire him.
He was despised and rejected by men;
    a man of sorrows, and acquainted with grief;
and as one from whom men hide their faces
    he was despised, and we esteemed him not.

Surely he has borne our griefs
    and carried our sorrows;
yet we esteemed him stricken,
    smitten by God, and afflicted.
But he was pierced for our transgressions;
    he was crushed for our iniquities;
upon him was the chastisement that brought us peace,
and with his wounds we are healed.

Isaiah 53:1-5

Christian Focus Publications

Our mission statement –

STAYING FAITHFUL

In dependence upon God we seek to impact the world through literature faithful to His infallible Word, the Bible. Our aim is to ensure that the Lord Jesus Christ is presented as the only hope to obtain forgiveness of sin, live a useful life and look forward to heaven with Him.

Books in our adult range are published in four imprints:

CHRISTIAN FOCUS

Popular works including biographies, commentaries, basic doctrine and Christian living.

CHRISTIAN HERITAGE

Books representing some of the best material from the rich heritage of the church.

MENTOR

Books written at a level suitable for Bible College and seminary students, pastors, and other serious readers. The imprint includes commentaries, doctrinal studies, examination of current issues and church history.

CF4•K

Children's books for quality Bible teaching and for all age groups: Sunday school curriculum, puzzle and activity books; personal and family devotional titles, biographies and inspirational stories – because you are never too young to know Jesus!

Christian Focus Publications Ltd,
Geanies House, Fearn, Ross-shire,
IV20 1TW, Scotland, United Kingdom.
www.christianfocus.com
blog.christianfocus.com